Homosexuality

What Does It Mean?

By Julie K. Endersbe, MEd

Consultant:
B. R. Simon Rosser, PhD, MPH, LP
Associate Professor
Program in Human Sexuality
Department of Family Practice and Community Health
University of Minnesota Medical School

LifeMatters
an imprint of Capstone Press
Mankato, Minnesota

LifeMatters books are published by Capstone Press
818 North Willow Street • Mankato, Minnesota 56001
http://www.capstone-press.com

Printed in the United States of America

Library of Congress Cataloging-in-Publication Data
Homosexuality: what does it mean? / by Julie Endersbe
         p.   cm. — (Perspectives on healthy sexuality)
    Includes bibliographical references and index.
    Summary: Provides an overview of sexuality and sexual orientation
    and discusses the issues and concerns of teenage homosexuals,
    including coming out, support systems, risks, fears, prejudices, and
    healthy sexual behavior.
    ISBN 0-7368-0275-4 (book). — ISBN 0-7368-0293-2 (series)
    1. Homosexuality Juvenile literature. 2. Gay youth Juvenile
    Literature. 3. Teenagers—Sexual behavior Juvenile literature.
    4. Coming out (Sexual orientation) Juvenile literature.
    [1. Homosexuality.] I. Title. II. Series: Endersbe, Julie.
    Perspectives on healthy sexuality.
    HQ76.26.E53   2000
    306.76´6—dc21   99-31422
                                                         CIP

Staff Credits
Anne Heller, editor; Adam Lazar, designer; Heidi Schoof, photo researcher

Photo Credits
Cover: UP Magazine/©Tim Yoon
FPG International/©Ron Chapple, 45
Index Stock Photography/15, 16, 30, 43
International Stock/©Dusty Willison, 28; ©Peter Langone, 51
PhotoDisc/©Barbara Penoyar, 6
Photri/25
Unicorn Stock Photos/©Jeff Greenberg, 9; ©Aneal F. Vohra, 11; ©Tom McCarthy, 32; ©Steve Bourgeois, 38
Uniphoto, Inc./©Bob Daemmrich, 57
UP Magazine/©Tim Yoon, 20, 54, 59

Table of Contents

Chapter Overview

Sexuality is complex. Attitudes are an important part of sexuality.

Sexual orientation is sexual attractions to other males and females. Attractions to individuals of the opposite sex are called heterosexual. Attractions to individuals of the same sex are called homosexual. Attractions to both sexes are called bisexual.

Learning about who you are attracted to and having words to describe those attractions are important challenges for all teens. Another important challenge is accepting your sexuality.

Chapter 1

Sexuality and Sexual Orientation

My sexuality has always been tough for me. I had few positive role models for it. I didn't know anybody who was gay.

Kyle, Age 19

My aunt actually helped me to understand my sexuality. She had a really healthy relationship with my uncle. They openly loved each other, yet they were very individual. I wanted that kind of openness and individuality in a partner. I wanted a long-term loving relationship.

When I met Philip, I was able to talk with him about my expectations. We both talked about what we wanted from a relationship. Right now we choose not to be sexually active. There's so much I'm still trying to understand about my sexuality. I think our discussions are helpful in understanding our individual sexuality.

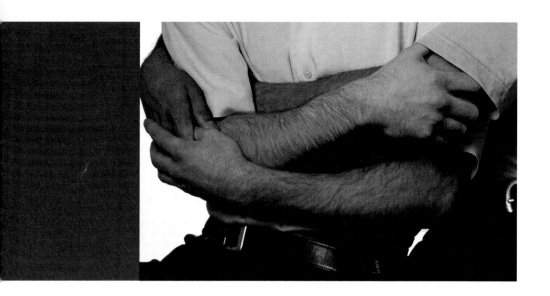

Attitudes and Feelings About Sexuality

Human sexuality is a wonderful part of life. It makes us feel alive. It helps us to fall in love and express ourselves as sexual beings. Understanding and valuing sexuality are important.

Part of understanding sexuality is knowing your body and how it responds sexually. When most people think about sex, they think about intercourse. However, penetration of the penis into the vagina, anus, or mouth is just part of sexuality. Sexuality also is about touching, kissing, and masturbation, or rubbing the genitals for pleasure. It is about feeling sexy inside and feeling good about your attractions.

Your attitudes and feelings are an important part of sexuality. This includes what you think is right and wrong about sexuality. It includes knowing yourself and your sexual attractions. It also includes being comfortable with your sexual orientation.

The terms *heterosexuality* and *homosexuality* did not exist before 1890.

Sexual preference is a term once used to describe sexual orientation. Sexual orientation is no longer believed to be a preference or choice.

Did You Know?

Sexual Orientation

Sexual orientation refers to sexual attractions to other people as males and females. Opposite-sex attractions and behaviors are called heterosexual. Same-sex attractions and behaviors are called homosexual. Some people are attracted to and have sex with both males and females. This is called bisexual orientation. Some people do not feel much attraction at all or do not have sex with others. This is called asexual orientation. All four orientations are normal.

People attracted to the opposite sex usually call themselves heterosexual or straight. Males attracted to other males usually call themselves gay. Females who are attracted to other females usually call themselves lesbian. Part of adolescence is learning about who you are attracted to. Part of it also is having words to describe your attractions.

Having sex with the same gender—male or female—doesn't make you homosexual. Likewise, having sex with the opposite gender doesn't make you straight. Many adolescents experiment with having sex with others. This experimentation allows teens to work out what is right for them. Being gay, bisexual, lesbian, or heterosexual is about who people desire and are likely to love. It is not so much about who they may have experimented with.

Fast Fact

Some studies indicate 1 in 10 people have a homosexual orientation. That equals about 25 million Americans.

Some people confuse sexual orientation with gender. Most people of any sexual orientation like their gender as it is. It's a myth that all gay males have female characteristics or that all lesbian females have male characteristics. However, some males feel like they are women, and some females feel like they are men. These people are called transsexual.

Experts still don't know what determines a person's sexual orientation. However, they do know it is not a choice. Sexual orientation appears to be set early in life, probably by age eight.

The Development of Sexuality

Even before we're born, our sexuality is developing. Some aspects of sexuality such as gender are inherited. Therefore, some aspects of our sexuality are already in place by the time we're born. We are all born with the capacity to be sexual.

Early in life, children learn from their parents what it means to be male or female. Even before birth, babies explore their body and genitals. Children may masturbate. Masturbation is a way to discover the sexual pleasures of the body and learn about attractions.

Puberty usually begins around ages 9 to 11. During puberty, the adolescent body begins to produce hormones. These hormones prepare the body for adulthood, sexual activity, and reproduction, or having a child. Girls typically begin puberty earlier than boys do.

Sexual desire increases during puberty. The production of hormones fuels this sexual attraction to others. Teens often experience a variety of sexual attractions during puberty. It is common for some teens to have same-sex as well as opposite-sex attractions. A very intense attraction is called a crush.

Challenges for Gay and Lesbian Youth

Everybody is different when it comes to learning about sexual attractions. Some people know who they are attracted to and accept this. For others, learning about sexual attractions can be an important but confusing experience. Still others are not sure of their sexual attractions until they fall in love.

Fast Fact

Uncertainty about sexual orientation declines with age. Studies shows that 26 percent of 12-year-olds are unsure of their sexual orientation, but only 5 percent of 17-year-olds are unsure.

Like all teens, most gay and lesbian youth begin to recognize their sexual attractions. While sexual orientation appears to be set early in life, recognizing to whom we are attracted takes longer. Only about 20 percent of gay and bisexual males report knowing their sexual identity in junior high. Only about 6 percent of lesbian and bisexual females report knowing their sexual identity in junior high.

With support and good friends, many teens accept their gay or lesbian orientation without many problems. Because society pressures teens to be heterosexual, many gay and lesbian youth also may try heterosexual relationships. Accepting your sexual orientation takes time.

Cultural influences can affect how we think and feel about our sexuality. For example, some religions teach that homosexuality is wrong. This can be especially hurtful and confusing for gay or lesbian youth. Some may not know anyone else who is gay or lesbian. They may feel very lonely and alone.

It's important for gay and lesbian youth to find others whom they can trust. Everyone needs an understanding person to talk with. All of us need to learn to recognize and freely express our feelings. Most heterosexual teens share information with friends or family about dates and their latest crush. In the same way, gay and lesbian teens need others who will listen. However, they may need extra support from adults and friends because of prejudice.

Points to Consider

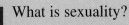

What is sexuality?

What are some kinds of sexual orientation?

Why is it important to accept your sexual orientation?

Chapter Overview

Sexual health is an important part of everyone's health.

Having pride in your identity is a big part of good sexual health.

Sex between males, between females, or between a male and a female is more similar than different.

Chapter 2

Developing a Healthy Sexuality

Part of being a healthy sexual person is knowing your attractions and being comfortable with who you are. In fact, gay and lesbian people have taught researchers some important things. They have taught that pride in a person's identity is an important part of sexual health. They also have shown the importance of knowing yourself and feeling good about who you are.

Fast Fact

A large study was done with high school students. It showed that 88 percent of students described themselves as mostly heterosexual, 1 percent as mostly homosexual, and 11 percent as unsure.

People learn healthy sexuality in various ways. Some teens learn best by doing or experimenting. Others decide to wait for that special person to come along. Some teens learn by looking at pictures or dreaming about what they want, sometimes while masturbating. Others learn by asking questions, talking with friends, trying out different attitudes and behaviors, reading books, or watching movies.

Whatever your sexuality may be, learning who you are sexually is a gradual process. Learning to appreciate your sexual identity is part of that process. The process happens over several years.

Sexual Self-Esteem

Many teens have concerns about their body. Good sexual self-esteem includes accepting your body the way it is. After all, having a perfect body is impossible. It's also not necessary to have a perfect body to be healthy or happy. Good self-esteem includes a healthy self-respect. It includes appreciating the beauty of your body just as it is.

When I was growing up, it seemed like sexuality was some unclear idea that **Roberta, Age 17** nobody could define. I know a lot of my friends had a hard time dealing with growing up and sex and stuff. I got most of my information from books.

I wanted a sexual relationship with a certain girl. At the same time, I didn't really know what I was supposed to do. Books give limited ideas on this. I wished I knew how to approach her. Or I wished I had someone to talk with about it.

Sexual Behavior

Part of healthy sexuality is knowing what you like to do sexually. It also is respecting that knowledge and going at your own pace. You should never feel forced or pressured to have sex. For this reason, many gay, lesbian, bisexual, or heterosexual teens choose not to rush into intercourse. They would rather wait until they meet that special person or have dated a partner for a while. This allows them the chance to get to know the person well before engaging in sex.

In sex, most people like to start by kissing, touching, stroking, and talking. Most male-male sex and female-female sex involves mutual masturbation and body rubbing. This is safe and pleasurable. Many people also enjoy oral sex. They kiss, lick, and suck the other person's penis or vagina. They also may enjoy receiving the same pleasure from their partner.

Sex doesn't have to involve intercourse. For example, about one in every three gay men prefer not to engage in anal sex. Similarly, some lesbian females prefer oral sex and mutual masturbation to being entered. Other gay and lesbian people may use sex toys to satisfy each other.

Many teens who feel they may be gay or lesbian can feel pressure to engage in penile-vaginal sex. For most gay and lesbian teens, this is the same pressure most teens feel to "do it." In fact, most teens of all sexual orientations have tried intercourse by age 19. Some gay and lesbian teens try penile-vaginal sex, hoping to change their sexual orientation. This doesn't make them change.

In some American Indian cultures, having a same-sex attraction was called being Two-Spirited. The tribe honored such people as having special gifts and being especially blessed.

First Relationships

At some stage, most teens want to fall in love. Gay and lesbian teens are the same. However, finding that special someone can present challenges. They face important questions such as where they can go to meet others like themselves. They wonder how to date and when to begin being sexual. They want to know what to do sexually. Another important question is whether you want someone you like just as a friend or as a possible lover. It can become very confusing if you don't work out the distinction between friend or lover.

Points to Consider

When should a person engage in sex?

What do you think are good ways to learn about different kinds of sexuality?

What qualities are you looking for in a boyfriend or girlfriend?

Chapter Overview

Coming out is the process of accepting one's homosexuality and sharing it with others.

Some gay and lesbian youth prefer not to come out until they are older. Comfort with and acceptance of a person's sexual identity take time.

Being honest with yourself and building a safe support system are important parts of sexual health.

Chapter 3

Coming Out

Coming out is the process of naming, valuing, and celebrating your sexual identity. The phrase "coming out" is used because hiding one's sexual identity "in the closet" is like pretending it's not there. The gay and lesbian community made the phrase "coming out" popular. Now other groups use the phrase to help them value and reclaim important parts of themselves.

Choosing when to come out and being honest with yourself are important. Some adolescents may choose not to come out until they are self-sufficient or have left home. Others decide that it is best just to be out. They find this is healthier than dealing with the negative feelings of living in the closet.

Should I Come Out?

Adolescence can be a difficult time for many gay and lesbian teens. There is no one right way to handle coming out. Many teens prefer to focus on other areas of their life like school, sports, and friendships. They come out when they are older. Others may tell one or two trusted people in order to build their support system. Some teens tell everyone.

Coming out is never easy. It takes courage and belief in yourself to stand up for who you are. It takes trust and maturity in knowing who to tell and not to tell. You need to be able to handle the other person's reaction. For example, some parents are very accepting. They already may have guessed and are waiting for their child to come out to them. Other parents, however, cannot immediately accept that their child is gay or lesbian. Some teens have been kicked out of their home or have lost friends. It is important to have a plan for handling rejection before coming out to others.

"When I come out to someone, I make sure I keep talking for a bit. This gives the other person a chance to absorb what I've just said without putting pressure on him or her to respond right away."
—Adam, age 17

Asking Important Questions

When deciding who to come out to, it's important to ask the following questions:

Am I knowledgeable about being gay or lesbian? Do I know enough to answer another person's questions?

Do I feel ready to share this information about myself with someone?

What is my plan if the other person cannot accept this information?

Does the other person know people who are gay or lesbian? Do they accept them?

Why do I want to come out to this person?

Scientists have studied the relationship between coming out and mental health. Researchers could find no major mental health differences between heterosexual people and gay and lesbian people. Therefore, every major American medical association now recognizes that coming out can be a sign of mental health.

Building a Support System

Everyone needs good friends they can turn to and trust. Gay and lesbian teens also need to build a strong support system. A critical part of that support system is a safe person. Coming out to a safe person first may start to build confidence for coming out to others. A safe person may have these qualities:

Listens without judging

Provides unconditional support

Provides challenges when necessary

Is accepting and open-minded

Respects sexual boundaries

Is knowledgeable about sexuality or knows of good resources

A teen can ask questions before coming out to someone to test if the person is accepting. For example, a teen can ask how someone feels about homosexuality. How someone answers this question may help show how accepting the person will be.

Surrounding yourself with a support system makes it easier to be yourself. It also provides a safe outlet for sharing feelings and getting guidance. Chapter 4 further describes support systems for gay or lesbian youth.

Understanding sexual identity takes time. Not all gay and lesbian teens go through the same process in coming out. However, these are some common stages that many people go through.

1. Confusion—Most people, gay or straight, start out feeling confused about their sexuality. They may feel different and hope these feelings go away. They may wonder why they are not more attracted to the opposite sex. Counseling can help teens work through this confusion to understand their feelings better.

2. Comparison—In this stage, teens start to accept that homosexual feelings are part of themselves. However, many try to pass as heterosexual because of the pressure to be heterosexual. They may date the opposite sex, and some may get involved sexually. In fact, all teens compare themselves with other teens. At this stage, however, gay and lesbian teens frequently feel very different from heterosexual teens. They may feel like something is wrong with them. A good support system and counseling can help to get through this stage.

3. Tolerance—In this stage, gay and lesbian teens begin to accept that their same-sex feelings are not going away. The coming-out process starts with being honest with oneself. In this stage, it's important to start meeting other gay and lesbian people who feel the same way. This helps to reduce the feelings of confusion and loneliness. Positive experiences help teens to move from tolerating their sexuality to accepting it.

Several famous people were or are gay, lesbian, or bisexual by today's definition. Can you name what these famous people did or do?

Socrates	Julius Caesar	Elton John
Sappho	David Bowie	Alexander the Great
Shakespeare	Greg Louganis	Peter Tchaikovsky
Michelangelo	Alice B. Toklas	Rupert Everett
Gertrude Stein	Errol Flynn	Melissa Etheridge
Saint Augustine	Oscar Wilde	Martina Navratilova

4. Acceptance—With more contact, gay and lesbian youth come to accept their sexuality as normal. They accept that they are gay, lesbian, or bisexual. They start to tell other trustworthy people about who they are. However, it's still important to control who knows about their sexual identity. It may be important to keep that information from people who can hurt them.

5. Pride—In this stage, teens discover that their sexuality is good. They discover there are thousands of other gay and lesbian people. These people feel proud to be gay or lesbian. During this stage, teens feel a strong need to be with other gay and lesbian people. They become concerned about human rights for lesbian and gay people. Involvement in politics can be helpful.

6. Identity Synthesis—Eventually, pride gives way to seeing the good and bad in all sexuality. Not all things associated with homosexuality are good. Not all heterosexual people are prejudiced. In this stage, gay and lesbian teens can appreciate their sexuality. It is an important gift that is one part of their larger identity. They are free to choose whom to tell about themselves.

Points to Consider

What does the phrase "coming out" mean?

What should a gay, lesbian, or bisexual teen consider before coming out to family and friends?

Do you have a safe person in your life? What qualities make that person safe for you?

What is your support system like? How could you build a stronger support system?

Chapter Overview

Support systems are the people in your life who care about you. They may include family, relatives, friends, and paid professionals.

Parents vary in their understanding of sexual orientation. Even so, they can be an important part of a support system.

Sharing personal information with paid professionals can be a safe choice.

An ideal support system includes some people with the same sexual orientation as yours.

Chapter 4

Support Systems

Support systems are important for all teens because everyone needs people who care. These systems are especially important for gay and lesbian youth. A strong support system helps to face challenges and to lower stress and anxiety. If some people are not supportive, it is important to keep searching to find people who are.

I was real nervous before talking with my **Aimee, Age 17** dad about being lesbian. He and I had always been close because we had some things in common. We loved to hang out together. But we never talked too much about serious stuff. Late one night I told him I was a lesbian. He just kissed me and gave me a hug.

The next morning he said, "I want you to be happy. It's your job to be the best person you can be. I will do all I can to help you be that person." It was beyond what I could have imagined. Sometimes I wish I had talked with him sooner.

Parents

Parents are an important part of a teen's support system. Unfortunately, not all parents are knowledgeable about sexuality. This means that some parents may not know how to deal with their child's homosexuality. Most teens need and want to be honest with their parents as well as to have their support. Teens who have a good relationship with their parents should think about including them in their support system.

Gays and lesbians are a minority. Unlike other minorities, they don't share being a part of a minority group with their parents. This can affect the kind of support gay and lesbian teens receive from their parents.

Usually parents need time to accept their teen's sexual identity. It may have taken you several years to understand and appreciate who you are sexually. Your parents also may need time to understand and learn to appreciate this new information.

Sharing information about homosexuality is one step teens can take to educate their parents. Also, teens may encourage their parents to talk with a counselor. A group called Parents and Friends of Lesbians and Gays (PFLAG) is in almost every city. This group helps parents to learn from other parents about having a lesbian daughter or a gay son. In these ways, parents can develop an understanding of their teen's sexual identity. Teens and parents can build a support system that benefits both of them.

Sometimes parents react badly. Some choose hurtful words or actions. This can be heartbreaking for a gay or lesbian teen. The teen may choose to look elsewhere for support while parents move toward acceptance. Some parents may never accept their child's sexual identity. Just like their children, they may struggle with feeling guilty or ashamed about their child's sexuality.

Caring, Trusted Adults

A trusted adult can provide support that peers without experience may not be able to provide. Teens may look for caring, trusted adults among relatives such as aunts, uncles, or grandparents.

Some teens may choose a family. This means unrelated adults serve as substitute parents. They may serve as mentors, or people with experience who can give advice and teaching.

Almost all gay and lesbian people build a second "family" of gay and lesbian friends. These are supportive people with whom they hang out and can be open about themselves. Sometimes the parents of other gay and lesbian friends can provide helpful support.

Gay or lesbian adults make excellent support people. They have experienced the challenges of coming out. It's important to choose adults who will respect sexual boundaries and confidences and not try to take advantage.

"If you are a friend of someone who has told you he or she is homosexual, you might feel confused, upset, or worried. Try to deal with the news in a way that tells the person that you still love and care for him or her. Your friend trusted and respected you enough to confide in you. Your friend needs your love and understanding."
—Martha, age 16

Friends

Sharing sexual identity with friends can be risky. All teens struggle with defining and understanding their sexual identity. Telling friends about being gay or lesbian also may require educating them about sexuality.

It is important to ask yourself why you want to tell friends. It's also important to share your reasons when you tell them. For example, you may say you want support or help in understanding your feelings. Like parents and other adults, friends may need time to understand what being homosexual means.

Heterosexual friends may feel awkward. Some same-sex friends may fear you are attracted to them. Some heterosexual friends may feel you no longer want to do things with them. Some may fear others will think they are homosexual because they have a gay or lesbian friend. Some friends may even tell you not to tell others.

It can be especially hard to tell someone to whom you feel attracted. This is normal. However, it is important to be clear with the person: Being gay or lesbian does not automatically mean being attracted to everyone else of the same sex. If you have mixed feelings toward a best friend, first tell the person about yourself. Then later you can discuss how each of you feels about the friendship. It is good to have some friends with the same sexual orientation and interests as you do.

When teens come out to friends, new challenges can happen. Sometimes gay and lesbian teens need to stand up for themselves. This is to ensure they can do what their heterosexual friends do. For example, family occasions and school dances may feel lonely if you aren't allowed to bring a same-sex date. Explaining to others can help them understand. You can explain you are still the same person. It's just that you are likely to want to bring a same-sex partner to such events.

Professional Support

Some teens who are not sure about their sexuality and some gay and lesbian teens seek professionals for support. This can be helpful if you are feeling lonely or depressed or fear being rejected for your sexual orientation. Good professionals to talk with are a doctor, health care worker, teacher, or school counselor.

This nationwide toll-free number provides peer-counseling, information, and referrals. It is open Monday through Friday 6–10 P.M. and Saturday noon to 5 P.M. eastern time.

National Gay and Lesbian Hotline
1-888-843-4564

Did You Know?

Sharing personal information with paid professionals is usually a safe choice. A teen may be scared that the professional will tell others. The law requires most professionals to keep such information confidential.

Other Support

Gay, lesbian, bisexual, and questioning teens have other choices for support. Sometimes a school has certain teachers who provide extra support. Gay and lesbian hotlines provide support over the telephone. You don't have to give your real name. Some schools and communities have gay, lesbian, and bisexual teen support groups. Other communities have community centers, sports and social groups, and dances where teens can meet.

Points to Consider

Why are support systems important to gay or lesbian youth?

What kinds of people make up a support system?

How might a gay or lesbian teen feel sharing his or her sexual orientation with heterosexual teens?

What would you look for in an ideal support system?

Chapter Overview

Some gay, lesbian, bisexual, and questioning teens struggle with prejudice, depression, and thoughts of suicide.

Homophobia is an irrational fear of gay, lesbian, or bisexual people. It is based on myths or stereotypes and is a kind of prejudice.

Gay, lesbian, and bisexual youth may experience harassment at school. However, all youth have the right to attend school without being harassed.

Religion and spirituality are important to some teens. Finding a supportive religious community can help some gay or lesbian teens emotionally.

Chapter 5

Dealing With Emotions

Society accepts heterosexuality as normal. As a result, many people do not understand or accept homosexuality. Many people have strong opinions and even prejudice about homosexuality. This can be emotionally difficult for gay or lesbian youth.

Some teens may be so emotionally upset that they become depressed or consider suicide, or killing themselves. In fact, suicide attempts are three times higher among gay male youth than among straight males. Depression and suicidal thoughts usually disappear when teens get help, build a support system, and learn to value sexuality.

Some teens don't see that society is sometimes ignorant and cruel. Instead, they can feel like they are the problem because of their sexual attractions. This is called internalized homophobia.

One in five high school health teachers say that students in their classes often use abusive language when describing gay or lesbian people.

Homophobia

Homophobia is an irrational fear of gay, lesbian, or bisexual people. Internalized homophobia happens when people are scared inside of their own homosexual feelings. Homophobia is a kind of prejudice that is very painful to gay and lesbian teens. It can make people feel bad or even like something is wrong with them. Hurtful words and actions make accepting their sexual identity harder. Verbal, or spoken, harassment is destructive and painful.

School life can be particularly hard. Some straight teens are scared of facing sexuality issues. Others believe lies and myths about homosexuality. For some teens, it's important to fit in, to conform, or to bully those who threaten them. Some teens display or express hate in hallways, locker rooms, or the cafeteria. Many gay and lesbian teens report antigay jokes and being called a fag or dyke. The jokes and teasing can be especially hurtful.

Homophobia is based on myths and stereotypes, or overly simple opinions. For example, one myth is that gay or lesbian people molest or mistreat children. This is not true. In fact heterosexual males commit 95 percent of all sexual abuse of children.

"I have been called a faggot and a sissy all my life. It is easy for adults to say that I should just ignore it, and that is generally what they say. I have been hearing . . . my whole life . . . the saying 'sticks and stones will break my bones, but names will never hurt me.' But that isn't really true. Words do hurt me, and besides that I have been pushed, punched, and threatened."
—Anonymous in Cranston, Rhode Island

Fortunately, homophobia can be reduced or eliminated. Getting accurate information about sexuality and getting to know real gay and lesbian people decrease homophobia. Nobody needs to be told they are bad. Gay and lesbian teens may need to distance themselves from people who give them such messages.

Handling Emotions

Dealing with emotions surrounding homosexuality can be painful. Feelings of fear or rejection from peers can be stressful. Thoughts of suicide must be taken seriously. A positive support system and professional counseling can help a teen to deal with these thoughts.

Some teens feel so hopeless that they leave home. Others may drop out of school rather than face the harassment. However, both leaving home and dropping out of school lead to additional problems. Professional counselors and a good support system can help teens stand up against harassment. This can help to improve home and school life for gay and lesbian teens.

Graduating from high school is important for future opportunities. Therefore, some teens decide to report harassment to school principals and teachers. Others decide to change schools or attend alternative learning centers. All youth have a right to education. Federal laws forbid harassment in schools.

The Religious Community

Some religions teach that homosexuality is wrong. Some even offer groups that claim they can help people become heterosexual. Research shows that these groups do not work and can increase depression. The American Medical Association and the American Psychiatric Association both warn that trying to change sexual orientation can harm self-esteem.

Spirituality and religion often are an important part of life for gay and lesbian teens. Fortunately, some places of worship are accepting of gay people. There are places of worship that only gay and lesbian people attend.

Teens looking for support from the clergy can ask such questions as "What do you think about homosexuality?" Answers to these questions determine whether someone is a safe person with whom to talk. If the person isn't knowledgeable about homosexuality, the teen can ask for a referral to someone who is.

Did You Know?

Difficulties with others accepting their sexual orientation is the primary reason that 40 to 50 percent of street youth have left home.

Points to Consider

Should teens put up with homophobia in schools? Why or why not?

How does homophobia affect gay and lesbian teens?

What are three things a teen who is being harassed can do to stop the harassment?

Chapter Overview

Homosexual youth have an increased risk for substance abuse.

Gay, lesbian, and bisexual teens can be so hungry for acceptance and love that they risk having sex without protection.

Sexually transmitted diseases (STDs), including HIV, are spread through sexual contact with an infected person.

Early detection and treatment as well as protected sex are necessary to prevent the spread of STDs.

Chapter 6

Dealing With Physical Risks

Everyone desires acceptance and love. When people are made to feel different, this desire can be even stronger. This desire leads some teens to take risks with their body. For example, they may already know that having unprotected sex can lead to a sexually transmitted disease (STD). They may already know that using alcohol and other drugs can impair their judgment. However, they may be willing to take the risks because they want to be accepted.

Gay or lesbian teens are 50 percent more likely to use alcohol and 3 times more likely to use marijuana than heterosexual teens.

Drug Abuse

Teens who are under stress may use drinking and other drugs as an escape. Alcohol and other drugs negatively affect the mind and body. For example, alcohol is a depressant. It can make feelings of doubt and worthlessness worse. As drug use increases, it leads to addictions and risks with unprotected sex. Using alcohol and other drugs as an escape only makes matters worse.

Gay and Lesbian Places and Activities

In some cities, gay bars and nightclubs have teen nights when teens are welcome but cannot drink alcohol. Some teens may try to sneak into gay bars. They do this to meet other gay and lesbian people. They feel they can be themselves in these places and feel good about their sexuality. However, bars and nightclubs also carry some risks.

Most gay and lesbian people do not molest, or mistreat, minors. Some adults, however, use bars to take advantage of youth sexually. This risk increases when alcohol and other drugs are used. This is because drugs and alcohol blur thinking and the ability to maintain boundaries. A teen who feels like experimenting sexually is wise to do so with someone who is the same age emotionally and physically. If a teen decides to go to a gay bar, it's a good idea to go with friends.

There are alternatives to gay bars. Such places are gay and lesbian houses of worship, sports groups, or coffee shops. Teens also can participate in Pride marches, AIDS walks, gay community celebrations, and gay and lesbian choruses.

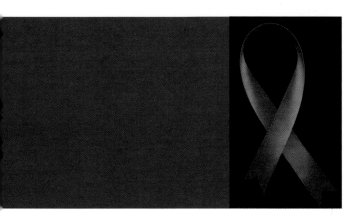

Sexually Transmitted Diseases

Some teens take chances and engage in unprotected sex. They also may have multiple partners. These two risks together put teens at the greatest risk of getting STDs. Male teens who have sex with other males are the highest risk group for STDs. Lesbian and bisexual teens who sometimes have sex with males also are at high risk.

STDs are spread through sexual contact with a person who already has an infection. They are spread through exchange of body fluids during penile-vaginal or penile-anal intercourse. Body fluids such as vaginal secretions and semen carry the germs.

STDs also can be spread in other ways. Drug users who share needles risk transmitting HIV, hepatitis, and other STDs. Needles used on more than one person for body piercing or tattooing can transmit HIV and hepatitis. Hepatitis and other STDs can be transmitted during oral-anal sex. People who have sores or cuts in their mouth can get STDs through oral sex.

Many STDs continue to spread because they have no symptoms. As a result, it is difficult to tell by looking at people who is infected. Many times people don't realize they have an STD and can unknowingly spread it.

Myth: HIV is a gay disease.

Fact: Worldwide, HIV is most commonly spread between heterosexuals.

Two of the most serious STDs are HIV and hepatitis.

HIV and AIDS

Human immunodeficiency virus (HIV) is a deadly STD. HIV is the leading cause of death for young American men who have sex with men. It also is a leading cause of death for young women. Some researchers believe about 80 percent of these deaths result from transmission of HIV during adolescence. Two ways HIV is spread are unprotected penile-vaginal and penile-anal sex.

HIV is a tiny virus that invades the body and destroys the immune system. The immune system's main job is to protect the body from illness. Over time, HIV weakens the immune system until the body can't fight diseases. At this point, acquired immune deficiency syndrome (AIDS) develops. Everyone needs to take HIV seriously.

Other STDs

Hepatitis B, genital herpes, and genital warts are all STDs caused by different viruses. These viruses stay in the body for life. These STDs can all be treated but not cured. Among these STDs, hepatitis is of most concern. It can lead to serious health problems or death. Hepatitis is the only STD that can be prevented with a vaccine. All sexually active teens should get the hepatitis vaccination.

Different bacteria cause STDs such as chlamydia, gonorrhea, and syphilis. These STDs can be cured with an antibiotic if they are detected and treated early. If these infections are not treated, they also can cause serious health problems or death.

Tests and Prevention

Regular health checks and tests are important for finding STDs. Early treatment can prevent more serious problems. Specific tests can detect the different STDs. Tests are especially important, because many people have no symptoms, or evidence, of an STD. All sexually active people should be tested for STDs once a year. They also should be tested each time they have a new sexual partner.

It is important to see a doctor immediately if there is any suspicion of an STD. Testing is the only way to know for sure if a person has an STD. Sexually active gay and lesbian teens should mention to the doctor that they are sexually active. They also should tell the doctor that they are gay or lesbian.

Using protection during sexual activity is perhaps the most important way to prevent STDs. Chapter 7 provides more information about protected, or safer, sex.

Points to Consider

Why do some teens take risks with alcohol and other drugs or sexual activity?

What are some important questions to ask yourself before becoming sexually active?

Why do you think it is important for gay or lesbian teens to share their sexual orientation with their doctor?

Chapter Overview

There is no one right age to become sexually active.

Monogamy is a healthy standard in a relationship. It is a mutual commitment between two people.

Protective barriers prevent the spread of STDs.

Part of being sexually active is setting sexual limits. Healthy sexuality includes being able to communicate about sex and your sexual history and to respect one another's limits.

Chapter 7

Safer Sex

Safer sex is important for everyone, especially teens who are thinking about becoming sexually active. There are other considerations to make before becoming sexually active. Those who choose to be sexually active should think about precautions. Some precautions include outercourse, monogamy, and using protection during intercourse.

Becoming Sexually Active

Because each person is different, there is no one right age for gay and lesbian youth to become sexually active. Some teens prefer to wait until they are older. Others feel ready and want to experiment. Some are so hungry for love that they try to meet this need through sex.

Before becoming sexually active, it's important for a teen to answer these questions:

What kind of sex do I want or not want? What are my sexual boundaries?

Do I know enough about sex, safer sex, and how to protect myself?

Do I have enough self-esteem and assertiveness to insist on using safer sex every time?

With whom do I want to have sex? What does that person want?

Can I say no if I don't want to have sex with someone?

Some people use sex to try to make themselves feel better. Like alcohol and drugs, however, casual sex is not a solution. If a teen is using sex to feel better, it's important to do two things: use protection and seek help. Teens with good self-esteem are less likely to use sex to mask their problems. They are more likely to insist on using protection if they are sexually active.

Brandon, Age 17

I get very few chances to date in my town. Even when I do, it's at some far-away place. I'm always looking over my shoulder. I'm only out to my uncle. So what do I do with my desire to have sex?

I know I'm not ready to have sex. I've read too much about HIV and hepatitis. Still I have condoms at home. I am preparing myself. I want to be prepared when the time comes. I want my first sexual relationship to be special and safe. I won't risk my life for some quick sexual encounter.

Outercourse

Outercourse is sexual play without intercourse. It can provide sexual satisfaction for partners with little risk of spreading STDs. It can be fun and helps couples learn about each other. Outercourse may include hugs, hand holding, touching, deep kissing, or mutual masturbation. It may include petting above or below the waist, body rubbing, or kissing the genitals. Outercourse is the most common form of sex between males and between females.

Outercourse requires communication and commitment. Part of good sexual communication is being able to talk about what you like. It also is showing a partner how you like to be touched. Setting limits and committing to maintain those limits are important. Also, partners should be prepared with protection in case they change their mind.

Monogamy

In monogamy, two people choose to have a sexual relationship only with each other. Monogamous relationships also are called closed. Monogamy is a safe choice for teens emotionally and physically. It can strengthen a relationship by building communication, trust, and safety between partners.

Serial monogamy means each relationship has a long-term commitment. For example, Cal dates Jim for eight months. Next, Cal dates Todd for a year. During his periods of dating, Cal only has sex with his current partner. Protection is still important unless both partners have tested negative for HIV and other STDs.

Protected Sex

Protected sexual intercourse is having sex using a barrier. These protective shields prevent the exchange of body fluids and reduce the spread of STDs. Every sexually active teen needs to protect his or her body from infected body fluids. Condoms and dental dams are two types of protection.

Condoms

Male condoms are thin latex rubber or polyurethane material designed to cover a penis and collect semen. Using a condom during intercourse is 10,000 times safer than not using a condom. Latex or polyurethane condoms for intercourse are far more effective than lambskin condoms.

Female condoms are small bag-like pieces of polyurethane that either males or females can use. They fit inside the vagina or anus to keep out infected body fluids.

Both male and female condoms take practice for proper use. Male teens who have not used condoms before can practice putting one on while masturbating.

Lubricants are usually necessary when using condoms. Lubricants add moisture and sensation and ease movement during intercourse. Without lubricants, intercourse can be painful. Only water-based lubricants should be used with latex condoms. These lubricants are available in most drugstores. Lubricants such as cooking and massage oil and hand or body lotions contain oils that break down condoms. Therefore, these other lubricants should not be used.

Dental Dams

Dental dams are made from a silky, thin latex material. They can be bought in most drugstores. A strong plastic kitchen wrap also can be used. During oral sex involving the vagina or rectum, the latex allows a person to lick and kiss through the dam. At the same time, it prevents the risk of exchanging infected body fluids.

Communication Between Partners

Communication between partners is an important part of sex. Partners communicate what they like or may like to try. For safer sex, it's important to insist on using condoms and to discuss each other's sexual history. Partners should communicate any history of STDs or HIV. They also should communicate about their limits and the types of protection they use. They need to do this before any sexual contact.

Points to Consider

Why is unprotected sexual intercourse risky?

What are some good reasons to choose to have or not to have sex?

Why is it important to know how to use a condom before you actually need one?

Why is it important for sexual partners to communicate with each other?

Chapter Overview

A strong support system helps teens resolve questions about sexual identity.

Good self-esteem and assertiveness are part of healthy sexuality.

Practicing safer sex shows maturity and responsibility.

Willingness to accept responsibility for personal behavior is an important part of sexual readiness.

Once sexual standards are set, they should be respected.

Communication is an important part of any relationship. Partners need to communicate constantly.

Chapter 8

Healthy Sexuality—
Making It Work for You

A person's sexual identity develops over time and takes effort. Accepting and understanding one's sexual orientation is just one part of sexuality, and it is an important part. Gay, lesbian, and bisexual teens deserve to celebrate their sexuality. Learning to do this in a positive, healthy manner is a sign of maturity and sexual readiness.

High school seemed to pass in slow motion for me. I dreaded certain times of **Renaldo, Age 19** the day, especially gym class. I knew I was attracted to guys rather than girls. Kids started teasing me in the fourth grade. I wasn't interested in the same stuff the other boys were.

My parents pretty much saved me. They drove me to the city for art classes and science fairs. I took swimming lessons and learned to ride a horse. I played in a basketball league.

I like the person I am today. I still struggle with my sexual identity. It wasn't until college that I understood it better. I'm still in a learning stage. But I'm surrounded with good people. And I'm working hard to understand my sexuality better.

Accept Yourself

You can be your own biggest support. Learning to accept who you are as a person helps to build self-worth. You can try writing positive messages to yourself in a journal or on a mirror. You can find ways to celebrate your strengths and appreciate your individuality. You can be proud of who you are.

Michael Kaplan was 22 when he found out he had HIV. He was angry that there were not more places for gay, lesbian, bisexual, and transgender (GLBT) youth to meet and socialize in the Minneapolis-St. Paul area. So he founded District 202, a GLBT Youth Center run by and for youth. He got funding so teen HIV prevention workers could provide peer education. Today, District 202 is a national model showing how peer education works. It owns its own building and coffee shop. It has a softball team and support groups. It hosts dances and even a prom just for GLBT youth.

Know Yourself

Being gay or lesbian is as much about integrity, or completeness, as it is about sex. Knowing yourself, being honest about what you want sexually, and being true to yourself are important parts of sexual health. For example, some people want to experiment sexually with many different partners. They should not pretend to be monogamous. On the other hand, someone wanting a monogamous partner may choose to go slowly. The person may date someone several times before becoming sexually active. Both people need to share with their partners the sort of relationships they want.

Get to Know Your Community

Gay and lesbian teens are the future leaders of the gay community. Therefore, it is important to learn about gay and lesbian people in history and choose good role models. Gay and lesbian people are in all walks of life. They are doctors, lawyers, researchers, athletes, artists, politicians, and parents. Think about the sort of leader you want to be and the sort of life you want to lead. Then follow your dream.

"My school counselor kept telling me to read books. But I wanted more than words. I wanted to talk with someone. I didn't know a safe place to find that. Finally, I found a gay youth support group in my city. I went to a few meetings and learned a lot about where I'm at. I would highly recommend that gay or lesbian teens find a support group."
—Troy, age 17

Build Your Support System

A support system can help to minimize feelings of isolation and loneliness. Ideally, your support system includes some members of your family. It also may include neighbors, relatives, teachers, or trusted adult friends. Sometimes professional counselors can add another dimension to your support system. You can talk with other teens who share the same feelings. A gay, lesbian, and bisexual support group or hotline can provide information and resources. Reading about other gay or lesbian teens can help you to feel less alone.

Determine Your Readiness for a Sexual Relationship

Each person needs to determine his or her personal readiness for a sexual relationship. To be ready for an emotional and sexual relationship, you need to understand the risks and responsibilities involved. You must be prepared to use barriers each time you have sex. You need to able to communicate honestly and openly with your partner about each other's feelings. You need to be prepared to deal with rejection if a relationship ends.

All teens who are ready for a sexual relationship need to set limits on their personal sexual behavior. You need to know your limits before engaging in sexual activity. In setting your limits, you may want to think about these issues:

Will I take off any or all of my clothes?

What parts of my partner's body am I willing to kiss?

Will I allow someone to touch my genitals?

Can I tell or show a partner how I like to be touched?

What do I not want to do? Can I tell a partner what I don't want to do?

How and when will I talk about my sexual limits with my partner?

Set Your Sexual Standards

Sexual standards are part of healthy sexuality. These are the things you expect or want from a sexual relationship. Monogamy, practicing safer sex, and constant communication with your partner are all healthy standards. Knowing what you want and being able to share this knowledge also are important.

Did You Know?

All states have laws to protect minors who are exploited sexually by much older adults. These laws apply whether the adult is of the same or the opposite gender. They apply regardless of whether the minor wanted sex.

High sexual standards include choosing with whom to have a relationship. Violence, put-downs, and drug and alcohol abuse negatively affect relationships. Feeling pressured and settling for a partner whom you do not love also have negative effects. Healthy people do not stay in such relationships.

For teens, the age of a sexual partner is an important consideration. Some teens may be genuinely attracted to much older adults. However, it's healthier to choose a partner near your own age. Usually, the more two people have in common, the more likely the relationship is to succeed.

Practice Safer Sex

It is natural for teens to experiment with sexual activity. However, it is essential to make safe choices about protection during sexual activity. It is important to remember that not every sexual experience needs to end in intercourse. You need assertiveness to insist on safer sex every time and be ready to teach possible partners about safer sex.

Communicate With Your Partner

Truthful, honest communication is a vital part of any relationship. Communication gives relationships life and builds them. It also means partners talk about the good and the bad parts of their relationship. After all, no relationship is perfect.

Talking about sexual parts of a relationship also is important. Both partners need to be able to talk about what is working and what needs work to help the relationship to grow. Sometimes mistakes happen. For example, one partner may think the relationship is monogamous but the other partner doesn't. Without talking about such an issue, it won't be cleared up and may become more hurtful.

A sexual relationship should be mutual. Both partners should gain from the experience. If this does not happen, each partner is responsible to talk about it, to get help, or to end the relationship.

Points to Consider

What do you think are the most important parts of your sexual identity?

What do you like most about your sexuality?

What is important about maintaining your sexual standards once you have set them?

Why would it be beneficial to end a relationship that is hurtful and has no communication?

Glossary

abstinence (AB-stuh-nenss)—choosing not to have sexual relations

asexual (AY-sek-shoo-wuhl)—not sexual; not having sexual attractions or desires.

barriers (BA-ree-ur)—protective shields that prevent the exchange of body fluids during sexual activity

bisexual (bye-SEK-shoo-wuhl)—sexual attraction to both genders

coming out (KUHM-ing OUT)—the process of accepting oneself and sharing that knowledge with others

condom (KON-duhm)—a device that fits over the penis, inside the vagina, or inside the rectum to provide a barrier

dental dam (DEN-tuhl dam)—a flat sheet of latex used during oral sex to prevent exchange of body fluids

gay (GAY)—homosexual; usually refers to males who have homosexual attractions.

gender (JEN-dur)—the sex of a person; male, female, or transsexual.

genitals (JEN-i-tulz)—sex organs; the male sex organs are the penis and testes; the female sex organs are the clitoris and vagina.

homophobia (hoh-moh-FOE-bee-uh)—the irrational fear of homosexuality or homosexual people

homosexual (hoh-moh-SEK-shoo-wuhl)—relating to the desire for, attraction to, and/or sexual involvement with a person of the same gender

lesbian (LEZ-bee-uhn)—homosexual; usually refers to females who have homosexual attractions.

monogamy (muh-NOG-uh-mee)—an exclusive sexual relationship between only two people

sexual intercourse (SEK-shoo-wuhl IN-tur-korss)—penile-vaginal, penile-anal, or penile-oral sexual activity

sexual orientation (SEK-shoo-wuhl or-ee-uhn-TAY-shuhn)—sexual attractions, behavior, or desire for others based on the gender of the other person

For More Information

Bass, Ellen, and Kate Kaufman. *Free Your Mind: The Book for Gay, Lesbian, and Bisexual Youth and Their Allies.* New York: HarperCollins, 1996.

Due, Linnea. *Joining the Tribe: Growing Up Gay and Lesbian in the 90s.* New York: Anchor Books, 1995.

Pollack, Rachela, and Cheryl Schwartz. *The Journey Out: A Book for and About Gay, Lesbian and Bisexual Teens.* New York: Viking, 1995.

Reed, Rita. *Growing Up Gay: The Sorrows and Joys of Gay and Lesbian Adolescence.* New York: W.W. Norton, 1997.

Romesburg, Don (ed.). *Young, Gay, and Proud!* Boston: Alyson Publications, 1995.

Signorile, Michelangelo. *Outing Yourself: How to Come Out as Lesbian or Gay to Your Family, Friends, and Coworkers.* New York: Simon & Schuster, 1996.

Gay and Lesbian Youth Advocacy Council
55 Mason Street
San Francisco, CA 94102

National Gay Youth Network
PO Box 846
San Francisco, CA 94101

National Lesbian and Gay Health Foundation
1638 R Street Northwest, Suite 2
Washington, DC 20009

National Youth Advocacy Coalition
1711 Connecticut Avenue Northwest,
Suite 206
Washington, DC 20009-1139

PFLAG (Parents and Friends of Lesbians and
Gays)
11012 14th Street Northwest, #700
Washington, DC 20005
www.pflag.org

Alyson Publications, Inc.
www.alyson.com
Books for gay teens and others on political,
legal, financial, medical, spiritual, social, and
sexual issues

Canadian Gay, Lesbian & Bisexual Resource
Directory
www.gaycanada.com
Canada's community-based gay, lesbian, and
bisexual information network

Gay and Lesbian National Hotline
www.glnh.org
Describes services available and links to other
gay and lesbian hotlines

!OutProud!
www.outproud.org
Wide range of resources from the National
Coalition for Gay, Lesbian, Bisexual, and
Transgender Youth

National Runaway Hotline
1-800-621-4000
TDD: 1-800-621-0394

National Teen HIV/AIDS Hotline
(Fridays and Saturdays 6 P.M.–12 A.M. eastern
time)
1-800-440-TEEN (8336)

National STD Hot Line
1-800-227-8922

Index